CONTENTS

The ADHD Playbook	1
Introduction: You Are Not Alone	3
Decoding ADHD: The Science Behind The Symptoms	5
The Neurobiology of ADHD	6
The Role of Genetics and Environment	7
Differentiating ADHD From Other Conditions	8
ADHD's Ripple Effect: Beyond Distractibility	10
Academic Challenges	11
Career Difficulties	12
Relationship Struggles	13
Everyday Life Impacts	14
Losing The Shame: Embracing Your Authentic Self	16
Facing Years of Negative Messages	17
Cultivating Self-Compassion and Acceptance	18
Recognizing the Strengths and Gifts of ADHD	19
Defining Your Own Success and Happiness	21
Taming The Chaos: Containment and Control Strategies	24
Why Containment Precedes Control	25
Physical Clutter	26
Mental Clutter	27
Incoming Tasks	28

Schedule and Obligations	29
Distractions and Hyperfocus	30
Smart-Phone Management	31
Reclaiming Your Time	32
Creating a System That Works: Principles and Tools	33
The Agile Manifesto	34
Getting Things Done (GTD)	35
Project Management	36
Inbox Zero	37
File Maintenance	38
Prioritization Strategies	39
Sustaining Your System	40
Tapping Into Your Superpowers: Leveraging ADHD Strengths	41
Creativity and Innovation	42
Hyperfocus and Flow	43
Intuition and Pattern Recognition	44
Resilience and Adaptability	45
Energy and Enthusiasm	46
Academic Mastery: Learning On Your Own Terms	49
Understanding Your Learning Style	50
Optimizing Your Study Environment	51
Effective Study Techniques	52
Time Management and Organization	53
Self-Advocacy and Support	54
Career Success: Finding Your Niche and Thriving	56
Identifying Your Passions and Strengths	57
Finding the Right Fit	58

Managing Tasks and Priorities	59
Maintaining Focus and Motivation	60
Improving Communication and Relationships	61
Harmonious Relationships: Connecting Authentically	63
Understanding How ADHD Affects Relationships	64
Cultivating Self-Awareness and Responsibility	65
Improving Communication and Emotional Connection	67
Managing Difficult Emotions and Conflicts	69
Building Trust and Reliability	71
Mastering the Everyday: From Finances to Fitness	73
Creating a Budget and Financial Plan	74
Organizing Your Home and Workspace	76
Prioritizing Self-Care and Wellness	78
Seeking Professional Support	80
ADHD Treatment: Finding What Works For You	82
Conventional Treatment Options	83
Stimulant Medication	84
Non-Stimulant Medication	86
Therapy	87
Alternative Treatment Options	89
Lifestyle Modifications	90
Mindfulness and Meditation	91
Omega-3 Fatty Acids	92
Neurofeedback	93
Building Your Treatment Plan	94
Conclusion: The Journey Continues	96
Additional Resources	99

THE ADHD PLAYBOOK
Embracing Your Unique Brain Wiring and Strategies for Success in Life, Work and Relationships

Gertrude Swanson

No part of this book may be reproduced or transmitted in any form whatsoever, electronic, or mechanical, including photocopying, recording, or by any informational storage or retrieval system without express permission from the author.

Copyright © 2024 JNR Publishing

All rights reserved

INTRODUCTION: YOU ARE NOT ALONE

If you have been diagnosed with Attention Deficit Hyperactivity Disorder (ADHD) as an adult, or suspect that you may have ADHD, you are far from alone. **The prevalence of ADHD in adults is estimated to be around 4.4% globally**, meaning that millions of adults worldwide are navigating life with this neurodevelopmental condition.

Despite its prevalence, ADHD in adults remains widely misunderstood and often goes unrecognized. Many people still associate ADHD primarily with hyperactive children, not realizing that the condition can persist into adulthood and manifest in different ways. **Common myths and misconceptions about adult ADHD abound**, such as the belief that it's just an excuse for laziness or irresponsibility, or that people with ADHD are unintelligent or incapable of success.

The reality is that ADHD is a complex neurological difference that affects individuals in varied ways. It is characterized by challenges with executive functioning skills such as attention regulation, working memory, impulse control, and task initiation. However, it's crucial to recognize that *having ADHD does not mean you are deficient or broken*. In fact, many people with ADHD possess incredible strengths and talents, such as creativity, intuition, resilience, and the ability to hyperfocus on their passions.

The key is learning to **embrace your unique brain wiring** and develop strategies to manage the challenges while leveraging your natural strengths. This book is designed to help you do just that. By gaining a deeper understanding of how ADHD affects you, building effective coping skills and support systems, and tapping into your innate potential, you can absolutely thrive with adult ADHD.

Throughout this comprehensive guide, we will explore the science behind ADHD symptoms, provide practical tools and techniques for navigating its impacts in various life areas, and empower you to cultivate self-compassion and define success on your own terms. You'll hear from real people who have transformed their lives by working with their ADHD, not against it.

Most importantly, this book aims to help you shed any shame or stigma you may carry about having ADHD. <u>You are not lazy, stupid, or incapable</u> - you simply have a brain that works a bit differently. By learning to understand, accept and even appreciate your ADHD brain, while developing personalized strategies that work for you, a fulfilling and successful life is absolutely within reach.

So let's dive in and begin this journey of thriving with adult ADHD together. In the next chapter, we'll start by examining the science and neurobiology behind ADHD to better understand how it shapes your mind and impacts your daily life. Remember, you are not alone in this - and with the right knowledge, tools and mindset, there's no limit to what you can achieve.

DECODING ADHD: THE SCIENCE BEHIND THE SYMPTOMS

To effectively manage ADHD and leverage its potential strengths, it's important to first understand the neurological underpinnings of the condition. While the exact causes of ADHD are not yet fully understood, decades of research have provided valuable insights into the brain differences and neurochemical factors involved.

THE NEUROBIOLOGY OF ADHD

At its core, ADHD is a disorder of **executive functioning**. Executive functions are a set of cognitive processes that enable us to plan, organize, initiate tasks, regulate emotions, and exercise self-control. In individuals with ADHD, several key brain regions involved in executive functioning appear to be structurally different and exhibit altered activity patterns compared to neurotypical brains.

One of the most significant neurological differences in ADHD is related to the neurotransmitter **dopamine**. Dopamine plays a crucial role in motivation, reward-seeking behavior, and the ability to sustain attention. Studies have shown that people with ADHD tend to have lower dopamine activity in certain brain areas, particularly the prefrontal cortex which is responsible for higher-order cognitive functions.

This reduced dopamine signaling may explain why individuals with ADHD often struggle with *working memory* (holding and manipulating information in mind), *attention regulation* (focusing on relevant stimuli while filtering out distractions), and *impulse control* (resisting urges and thinking before acting). The constant search for stimulation and novelty in ADHD can be seen as the brain's attempt to compensate for chronically low dopamine levels.

THE ROLE OF GENETICS AND ENVIRONMENT

Research indicates that ADHD has a strong genetic component, with heritability estimates ranging from 70-80%. If you have ADHD, chances are high that someone else in your family tree does as well. However, having the genetic predisposition does not guarantee that you will develop ADHD. Environmental factors, such as prenatal exposure to toxins, traumatic brain injuries, or highly stressful childhood experiences, are also thought to play a role in the emergence of ADHD symptoms.

It's likely that ADHD results from a complex interplay between genetic susceptibilities and environmental triggers that influence neurodevelopment. The exact combination of factors will vary from person to person, contributing to the diverse range of ADHD presentations.

DIFFERENTIATING ADHD FROM OTHER CONDITIONS

One challenge in diagnosing ADHD is that its symptoms can mimic or overlap with those of other mental health conditions. For example, difficulty concentrating can also be a symptom of depression, anxiety, or learning disorders. Impulsivity and emotional dysregulation are common in bipolar disorder and borderline personality disorder.

This is why a comprehensive evaluation by a qualified mental health professional is crucial for accurately identifying ADHD. Clinicians will look for a longstanding pattern of inattentive and/or hyperactive-impulsive symptoms that are pervasive across settings, begin in childhood, and cause significant impairment in daily functioning. They may use rating scales, cognitive tests, and in-depth interviews to determine if the diagnostic criteria for ADHD are met.

It's also important to note that ADHD frequently co-occurs with other psychiatric conditions. Over two-thirds of individuals with ADHD have at least one comorbid diagnosis, such as depression, anxiety disorders, substance use disorders, or learning disabilities. Comprehensive treatment must address these overlapping issues in conjunction with ADHD-specific interventions.

By understanding the neurobiological basis of ADHD and how

it manifests in your unique brain, you can start to reframe your symptoms as differences rather than deficits. In the next chapter, we'll explore how these core symptoms impact key areas of life such as academics, work, relationships, and overall daily functioning. Armed with this knowledge, you'll be better equipped to start building personalized strategies to navigate challenges and harness your strengths.

ADHD'S RIPPLE EFFECT: BEYOND DISTRACTIBILITY

While distractibility and inattention are hallmark symptoms of ADHD, the condition's impact extends far beyond occasional daydreaming or losing your keys. ADHD can have pervasive effects across major life areas, shaping your experiences in school, work, relationships, and day-to-day living. By recognizing these common challenges, you can start to develop targeted strategies to manage them more effectively.

ACADEMIC CHALLENGES

For many individuals with ADHD, academic difficulties first emerge in childhood but can persist or resurface in higher education and lifelong learning pursuits. Common struggles include:

- **Learning styles:** Traditional lecture-based instruction and rote memorization can be particularly challenging for ADHD brains that crave hands-on, interactive, and novelty-rich learning experiences.
- **Studying:** Sustaining attention while reading dense texts, taking effective notes, and organizing study materials can feel overwhelming, leading to inconsistent performance on exams.
- **Procrastination:** Difficulty initiating and persisting in tasks, especially those perceived as boring or challenging, often results in last-minute cramming sessions and missed deadlines.
- **Achieving goals:** Poor planning, time blindness, and distractibility can derail long-term projects and make it harder to break down ambitious goals into manageable steps.

CAREER DIFFICULTIES

ADHD's impact on executive functioning can lead to various challenges in the workplace, such as:

- **Finding the right fit:** Individuals with ADHD may struggle in roles that require sustained focus, strict adherence to routines, or heavy administrative duties. They often thrive in creative, fast-paced, and flexible work environments.
- **Managing tasks:** Prioritizing assignments, breaking down complex projects, and following through on commitments can be difficult with ADHD, potentially leading to missed deadlines and inconsistent performance.
- **Maintaining focus:** Open office plans, chatty coworkers, and constant digital distractions can exacerbate attention regulation challenges, making it harder to enter a state of deep work and productivity.
- **Advancing:** While individuals with ADHD often excel as creative problem-solvers and out-of-the-box thinkers, their struggle with organization and consistency may be mistaken for lack of motivation or competence, hindering professional advancement.

RELATIONSHIP STRUGGLES

ADHD can strain interpersonal connections, both romantic and platonic, due to difficulties with:

- **Communication:** Blurting out thoughts without a filter, interrupting others, or zoning out during conversations can lead to misunderstandings and hurt feelings.
- **Emotional regulation:** Impulsivity and low frustration tolerance can result in emotional outbursts, while rejection sensitive dysphoria (an extreme sensitivity to perceived criticism) can fuel conflicts.
- **Time management:** Consistently running late, underestimating how long tasks will take, and procrastinating on shared responsibilities can breed resentment in partnerships.
- **Responsibility:** Forgetting important dates, neglecting household chores, or impulsively agreeing to social commitments can make partners feel unappreciated and overburdened.

EVERYDAY LIFE IMPACTS

Beyond these major life domains, ADHD can affect your ability to effectively manage:

- **Finances:** Impulsive spending, forgetting to pay bills, and difficulty budgeting can lead to money worries and debt.
- **Organization:** Chronic disorganization and clutter in your physical space can increase stress and wasted time.
- **Sleep:** Insomnia, delayed sleep phase syndrome, and inconsistent sleep schedules are common in ADHD.
- **Health:** Difficulty maintaining regular exercise, healthy eating, and medication/appointment schedules can compromise well-being.
- **Self-care:** Losing track of self-care routines and hobbies can lower quality of life and provide less relief from stress.

The "Symptom Management Feedback Loop"

It's important to recognize that the relationship between ADHD symptoms and environmental challenges is bidirectional. Just as symptoms can make navigating certain situations more difficult, a poor fit between your brain and your surroundings can exacerbate ADHD symptoms in a vicious cycle.

For example, a highly distracting workplace with little accountability can worsen inattention and procrastination. A relationship in which criticism and blame dominate can heighten emotional dysregulation. A schedule that lacks routines and is overpacked with commitments can intensify organization and time management difficulties.

Breaking this feedback loop requires both developing effective symptom management strategies and shaping your environment to better accommodate your needs. By gaining insight into your unique pattern of strengths and challenges, you can start to craft personalized solutions to break out of vicious cycles and create more ADHD-friendly life structures.

In the next chapter, we'll dive deeper into the emotional component of thriving with ADHD by exploring ways to overcome internalized shame, reframe past difficulties, and embrace your authentic self with compassion and acceptance.

LOSING THE SHAME: EMBRACING YOUR AUTHENTIC SELF

One of the biggest barriers to thriving with adult ADHD is not the symptoms themselves, but the pervasive shame and negative self-image that often accompany them. Years of struggling to meet neurotypical expectations, facing criticism and misunderstanding from others, and internalizing societal stigma can leave deep emotional scars.

FACING YEARS OF NEGATIVE MESSAGES

From a young age, many individuals with ADHD are bombarded with negative messages about their abilities and character. Teachers may label them as "lazy," "disruptive," or "unmotivated" for their difficulties with attention and impulse control in the classroom. Parents may express frustration and disappointment over forgotten chores, impulsive behavior, or academic struggles. Peers may tease or exclude them for their social awkwardness or high energy levels.

Over time, these external judgments can become internalized as core beliefs about oneself. You may come to see yourself as fundamentally flawed, incapable, or unworthy. This toxic shame can fuel a vicious cycle of self-doubt, avoidance, and self-sabotage that keeps you stuck and unfulfilled.

CULTIVATING SELF-COMPASSION AND ACCEPTANCE

Breaking free from the shame spiral starts with learning to treat yourself with the same kindness, understanding, and acceptance you would extend to a good friend. This means:

- **Acknowledging your struggles:** Validate the very real challenges that ADHD has posed in your life, without judgment or minimization.
- **Reframing "failures":** View past difficulties not as personal deficits, but as the result of a poor fit between your brain and your environment.
- **Celebrating your successes:** Take time to acknowledge and savor your achievements, no matter how small they may seem.
- **Practicing self-forgiveness:** Let go of the need to be perfect and extend compassion to yourself in moments of struggle or setback.
- **Surrounding yourself with support:** Seek out people who understand and accept you as you are, while setting boundaries with those who feed into shame and self-doubt.

RECOGNIZING THE STRENGTHS AND GIFTS OF ADHD

An essential component of releasing shame is learning to embrace the positive qualities and abilities that come with your unique brain wiring. While ADHD certainly poses challenges, it can also confer distinct advantages, such as:

- **Creativity:** Unconventional thinking, a knack for novel solutions, and a vivid imagination.
- **Hyperfocus:** The ability to enter a state of intense concentration and productivity on tasks that captivate your interest.
- **Intuition:** A strong gut instinct, ability to read between the lines, and see the big picture.
- **Spontaneity:** A sense of adventure, openness to new experiences, and flexibility in the face of change.
- **Empathy:** A deep capacity for emotional attunement, compassion, and seeing multiple perspectives.
- **Resilience:** Resourcefulness in navigating challenges and bouncing back from setbacks.
- **Enthusiasm:** Infectious energy, passion, and excitement for ideas and interests.

Reframing "Failures" as Learning Opportunities

A key part of embracing your authentic self is learning to reframe perceived "failures" and missteps as valuable learning experiences. Instead of beating yourself up for a forgotten deadline, an impulsive decision, or a social faux pas, ask yourself:

- What can I learn from this experience?
- How can I use this information to make a different choice next time?
- What strategies or supports might have helped me navigate this situation better?
- How does this challenge reflect a mismatch between my needs and my environment, rather than a personal failing?

By shifting to a growth mindset and embracing imperfection as part of the human experience, you free up mental energy for problem-solving and self-discovery.

DEFINING YOUR OWN SUCCESS AND HAPPINESS

Ultimately, thriving with ADHD means letting go of external standards of success and defining your own path to fulfillment. This involves:

- **Clarifying your values:** Identifying what truly matters to you and aligning your life choices accordingly.
- **Setting authentic goals:** Pursuing aims that reflect your genuine desires and strengths, rather than what you feel you "should" want.
- **Celebrating your uniqueness:** Embracing your quirks, passions, and individual style as essential parts of who you are.
- **Finding your tribe:** Connecting with others who share your values, interests, and experiences for mutual support and belonging.
- **Practicing self-acceptance:** Extending unconditional positive regard to yourself, even as you work toward growth and change.

This process of self-discovery and self-acceptance is a lifelong journey. There will likely be times when old shame patterns resurface or when you find yourself slipping into comparison and self-judgment. The key is to meet these moments with compassion, reminding yourself that your worth is inherent and not contingent on your achievements or struggles.

As you learn to embrace your authentic self, you create space for true healing, growth and transformation. You start to view your ADHD not as a shameful defect, but as a unique facet of your identity that shapes your perceptions and interactions with the world. You recognize that your differences can be a source of strength and creativity, not just struggle.

With this foundation of self-acceptance in place, you are better equipped to build practical skills and strategies to manage the day-to-day challenges of ADHD. In the next section, we will explore how to create external structures and supports to contain the chaos, capitalize on your strengths, and craft a life that works with, not against, your natural wiring. Remember, releasing shame and embracing your authentic self is not a one-time event, but a daily practice of choosing compassion, courage, and connection. By committing to this practice, you open the door to a life of greater ease, joy, and fulfillment – ADHD and all.

Part II: Building a Solid Foundation

With a deeper understanding of ADHD's impacts and a growing sense of self-acceptance, you are ready to start building the practical skills and strategies to thrive with your unique brain. Just as a sturdy house requires a well-constructed foundation, creating a life that works with your ADHD means putting key structures and supports in place to manage symptoms and harness your strengths.

In this section, we will explore a range of tools and techniques to help you:

- Tame the chaos of physical and mental clutter through effective organization systems.

- Manage overwhelming tasks and competing demands with prioritization and time management strategies.
- Mitigate the impact of distractions and harness hyperfocus using technology and environmental modifications.
- Build a toolkit of planning and productivity strategies to achieve your goals with less stress and frustration.
- Identify and capitalize on your unique ADHD superpowers to create a life of meaning and purpose.

As you embark on this process, remember that building a solid foundation is an ongoing, iterative journey. What works for you may change over time as your circumstances and needs evolve. The goal is not to find a one-size-fits-all solution, but to cultivate a flexible and adaptable approach that honors your individual quirks and preferences.

It's also important to approach this process with self-compassion and patience. Developing new habits and skills takes time and practice, and setbacks are a normal part of the journey. Be kind to yourself as you experiment with different strategies, celebrate your successes along the way, and adjust course as needed.

With commitment, curiosity, and a spirit of self-discovery, you can absolutely create a solid foundation for a thriving life with ADHD. Let's dive in and start exploring the practical tools and techniques to make it happen.

TAMING THE CHAOS: CONTAINMENT AND CONTROL STRATEGIES

One of the hallmarks of ADHD is a sense of chronic disorganization and overwhelm. Piles of clutter, forgotten tasks, and a whirlwind of ideas can leave you feeling frazzled and paralyzed. The first step in building a solid foundation is learning to contain and control this chaos, both in your physical environment and your mental space.

WHY CONTAINMENT PRECEDES CONTROL

Many people with ADHD make the mistake of trying to tackle organization challenges with an all-or-nothing approach. They dive into ambitious plans to color-code their entire filing system or completely overhaul their schedule, only to abandon the effort when it proves unsustainable.

A more effective approach is to start with containment before moving on to control. Containment is about creating designated spaces and systems to hold the disorder, without demanding perfection. It's about finding ways to limit the chaos to manageable levels, so you can begin to establish control over your environment and your actions.

PHYSICAL CLUTTER

Physical clutter is often the most visible manifestation of ADHD-related disorganization. Papers, books, gadgets, and half-finished projects can quickly take over your space, leading to feelings of stress and overwhelm. Some strategies for containing physical clutter include:

- **Respecting and fearing the pile:** Acknowledge that piles are inevitable with ADHD, and that's okay. The goal is not to eliminate them entirely, but to keep them contained and manageable.
- **Using baskets and open storage:** Place baskets or trays in strategic locations to catch everyday items like mail, keys, and pocket contents. Open shelving can make it easier to see and access belongings.
- **Making closed storage accessible:** Reserve closed storage for infrequently used items. Label containers clearly and use transparent bins when possible to make contents visible.
- **Decluttering with Charity Pickup Services and Freecycle:** Schedule regular donation pickups to remove unwanted items from your space. Freecycle can also help you rehome clutter while keeping it out of landfills.

MENTAL CLUTTER

Mental clutter, or the constant swirl of thoughts, ideas, and worries, can be just as overwhelming as physical disarray. Some ways to contain mental clutter include:

- **"Potty Training" your brain:** Placing thought containers strategically throughout your environment to capture mental clutter. Notepads by the bed, voice memos in the car, and whiteboards in the office can all serve as receptacles for brain dumps.
- **Capturing ideas:** Use sticky notes, apps, or multi-colored index cards to jot down ideas and inspiration as they come to you. Sort and process these notes regularly to prevent mental backlog.
- **Specialized thought containers:** Create "Trouble Tickets" for nagging worries or problems. Write down the issue, potential solutions, and next steps on a dedicated notepad or document to clear mental space.
- **Maximizing writable surfaces:** Use dry-erase paint, chalkboard contact paper, or a giant wall calendar to capture ideas and reminders in high-visibility areas like the bathroom mirror or kitchen wall.

INCOMING TASKS

A constant influx of requests, assignments, and to-dos can quickly bury someone with ADHD. Taming task-related chaos requires systems for:

- **Minimizing incoming flow:** Unsubscribe from non-essential communications, filter solicitations, and set clear boundaries around your availability.
- **Managing email:** Use strategies like Inbox Zero, a dedicated "DMZ" folder for action items, and automatic filtering to keep email manageable.
- **Creating effective inboxes:** Set up physical trays or folders near entryways and work spaces to catch incoming paperwork, mail, and project materials. Process these inboxes regularly.

SCHEDULE AND OBLIGATIONS

Keeping track of appointments, deadlines, and commitments can feel like a full-time job with ADHD. Some strategies for containing schedule-related chaos include:

- **Kinkeeping:** Recognize the mental load of managing social and familial obligations. Delegate or automate what you can, such as using shared digital calendars or reminder services.
- **Digital calendar mastery:** Leverage features like color coding, multiple calendars, reminders, and recurring events to make your digital calendar system more ADHD-friendly.
- **Handwritten calendaring:** For tactile learners, a paper planner or bullet journal can be a grounding complement to digital tools. Create an index and use rapid logging to avoid overcomplicating the system.
- **Avoiding calendar overwhelm:** Be realistic about what you can commit to, and avoid scheduling based on wishful thinking. Block out ample time for transitions, self-care, and open space.

DISTRACTIONS AND HYPERFOCUS

Distractibility and hyperfocus are two sides of the ADHD coin that can wreak havoc on productivity. Some tips for containing their chaos include:

- **Identifying triggers:** Notice patterns around what distracts you and what sucks you into hyperfocus. External stimuli, certain tasks, and lack of movement are common culprits.
- **Setting boundaries:** Use visual timers, website blockers, and physical reminders like a "parking lot" for ideas to help you maintain boundaries around your attention.
- **Technology for focus:** Try apps like Freedom or Self Control to block digital distractions. Use noise-cancelling headphones and white noise to manage auditory stimuli.
- **Hyperfocus rescue remedy:** Have a designated friend, colleague, or family member on call to help break you out of hyperfocus with a text or call at agreed-upon intervals.

SMART-PHONE MANAGEMENT

Our pocket computers can be incredible tools for organization – or all-consuming distractions. Some smartphone containment strategies include:

- **App organization:** Group apps into folders by function or frequency of use. Keep temptations off the home screen and work-related apps visible.
- **Notification control:** Turn off all but the most essential notifications. Use Do Not Disturb liberally. Consider removing distracting apps from your phone entirely.
- **Home screen strategies:** Use a minimalist home screen to reduce decision fatigue. Consider a wallpaper with your top priorities as a regular reminder.
- **Phone containment:** Designate device-free times and locations, like the dinner table or bedroom. Use airplane mode or a "phone jail" to create distance when needed.

RECLAIMING YOUR TIME

One of the most profound costs of ADHD-related chaos is lost time. Spend a week tracking how much time you spend on distractions like social media, clutter-clearing, or procrastination to calculate their true cost. Then, gradually start replacing these time sinks with activities that energize and fulfill you, like hobbies, self-care, or quality time with loved ones. Remind yourself that every moment you reclaim from chaos, distraction, and overwhelm is a moment that you get to spend on what truly matters to you.

By implementing containment strategies in each of these areas, you can begin to tame the chaos of ADHD and make space for greater control and intentionality in your life. In the next chapter, we will explore how to use this foundation of containment to build a personalized productivity system that works with your brain, not against it.

CREATING A SYSTEM THAT WORKS: PRINCIPLES AND TOOLS

With the chaos of ADHD somewhat contained, you can now turn your attention to building a personalized productivity system to help you achieve your goals with less stress and frustration. An effective system will provide structure and support for your executive functions while also honoring your natural creativity and flexibility.

THE AGILE MANIFESTO

One approach to building an ADHD-friendly productivity system is to borrow principles from Agile, a project management methodology used in software development. The Agile Manifesto emphasizes:

- **Individuals and interactions over processes and tools:** Build systems around your strengths and preferences, not the other way around. No tool is one-size-fits-all.
- **Working solutions over comprehensive documentation:** Prioritize progress and learning through action over perfect planning. Get started and adjust as you go.
- **Customer collaboration over contract negotiation:** Involve key stakeholders (like your spouse, boss, or colleagues) in your productivity plans to ensure alignment and buy-in.
- **Responding to change over following a plan:** Embrace iteration and experimentation. If a system stops working, don't be afraid to scrap it and try something new.

GETTING THINGS DONE (GTD)

David Allen's Getting Things Done (GTD) methodology is another popular productivity system that can be adapted for ADHD brains. GTD involves five key steps:

1. **Capture:** Get everything out of your head and into an external system, whether it's a notebook, an app, or a voice memo.
2. **Clarify:** Process your inbox regularly, deciding what each item means and what (if any) action is required.
3. **Organize:** Sort action items by context, timeline, and priority. Park non-actionable items in a reference system or Someday/Maybe list.
4. **Reflect:** Review your system weekly to update lists, check progress, and make strategic decisions about what to prioritize.
5. **Engage:** Use your system to take action with confidence, knowing you're working on the right things at the right time.

GTD's emphasis on externalizing mental clutter and defining clear next actions can be particularly helpful for ADHD brains. However, it's important not to get bogged down in perfecting your system at the expense of actually getting things done.

PROJECT MANAGEMENT

For many people with ADHD, staying on top of multi-step projects is a major challenge. A few key strategies can help:

- **Choosing a tool:** Whether it's a digital app like Trello or Asana, a simple spreadsheet, or a paper-based bullet journal, find a project management tool that feels intuitive and visually appealing to you.
- **Defining projects:** In GTD parlance, a project is anything requiring more than one action step. Break projects down into concrete, manageable tasks.
- **Establishing contexts:** Assign each task a context based on the resources needed to complete it, such as location (home/office), equipment (phone/computer), or energy level (high focus/low focus).
- **Creating "Next Actions":** For each project, define the very next physical action required to move it forward. Be specific and granular, like "Email Sarah to ask for Q2 budget numbers."

INBOX ZERO

Taming the email beast is a perennial productivity challenge, but can be especially tricky with ADHD. Some tips for reaching Inbox Zero:

- **Process to empty:** Aim to process your inbox to zero at least once a week, making a decision about what each message requires.
- **Resist the urge to "just do it":** If a message requires an action that will take longer than 2 minutes, add it to your task management system instead of addressing it immediately.
- **Create an "Action" folder:** Move emails requiring a response or task to a dedicated "Action" folder, then process that folder regularly as part of your productivity system.
- **Use the DEA method:** Delete, Delegate, or Archive. If it's not actionable or reference-worthy, delete it. If it's something that can be delegated, forward it. Everything else gets archived.

FILE MAINTENANCE

Clutter and disorganization in your physical and digital filing systems can be a major stressor and time-waster. Some tips for keeping files manageable:

- **Make filing easy:** Use broad, intuitive categories and alphabetical order to make filing and retrieval more automatic. Resist the urge to create complex hierarchies.
- **Separate action from reference:** Keep your working files separate from your reference files. Use vertical files or trays for active papers, and file cabinets or binders for longer-term storage.
- **Go digital:** Scan documents whenever possible and save them to the cloud for easy search and retrieval. Use OCR software to make PDFs keyword-searchable.
- **Purge regularly:** Schedule a quarterly or annual purge of both paper and digital files. When in doubt, toss it out (or archive it to a backup drive).

PRIORITIZATION STRATEGIES

With so many competing demands on your time and attention, prioritization is key. Some strategies to try:

- **The Eisenhower Matrix:** Sort tasks into four quadrants based on urgency and importance. Focus on important-but-not-urgent tasks to avoid falling into constant firefighting mode.
- **Must/Should/Could:** Divide your to-do list into three categories: Must Do (non-negotiable), Should Do (important but not urgent), and Could Do (nice to have). Tackle your Must Dos first.
- **Structured Procrastination:** Leverage your inclination to procrastinate on high-priority tasks by always having a few less-important-but-still-worthwhile tasks on hand. You'll still be making progress, even if it's not on your top priorities.
- **Time-Blocking:** Divide your day into blocks of time dedicated to specific activities or types of tasks. Use a timer to stay on track, and build in breaks for transitions and recharging.

SUSTAINING YOUR SYSTEM

No productivity system is perfect, and even the best-laid plans will require troubleshooting and adjustment over time. Some tips for sustaining your system:

- **Notice red flags:** If you find yourself avoiding your system, falling behind on tasks, or feeling overwhelmed, take it as a sign that something needs to change.
- **Schedule regular reviews:** Set aside time each week (or at least monthly) to review your projects, next actions, and calendars. Use this time to celebrate progress, adjust plans, and identify areas for improvement.
- **Embrace iteration:** Your system will evolve as your life and needs change. Be open to experimenting with new tools and strategies, and don't be afraid to let go of what's not working.
- **Seek support:** Consider working with a coach or joining an accountability group to help you stay on track and troubleshoot challenges as they arise.

Remember, the goal of any productivity system is to reduce stress and overwhelm, not create more of it. Start small, be patient with yourself, and celebrate progress along the way.

With a foundation of solid routines and systems in place, you've created a launchpad for your innate creativity and strategic thinking abilities to take flight. In the next chapter, we'll explore how to leverage your unique ADHD brain and harness its superpowers for even greater success and fulfillment.

TAPPING INTO YOUR SUPERPOWERS: LEVERAGING ADHD STRENGTHS

While much of the conversation around ADHD focuses on its challenges, it's important to recognize and harness the unique strengths and abilities that come with this type of brain wiring. By tapping into your ADHD superpowers, you can not only overcome obstacles but also create a life of tremendous meaning, impact, and fulfillment.

CREATIVITY AND INNOVATION

One of the most remarkable gifts of the ADHD brain is its capacity for creativity and innovative thinking. Thanks to your ability to make novel connections, see patterns others miss, and think outside the box, you have the potential to be a visionary leader and problem-solver. Some ways to leverage your creativity include:

- **Divergent thinking:** Engage in brainstorming sessions where the goal is to generate as many ideas as possible, without judgment. Embrace wild and unconventional ideas.
- **Combinatory play:** Look for ways to combine seemingly unrelated ideas or concepts to create something new. Draw inspiration from diverse fields and experiences.
- **Constraint-driven creativity:** Embrace constraints as a source of creative inspiration. How might a limited budget, a tight deadline, or a specific set of materials spur innovative solutions?
- **Design thinking:** Apply your creativity to real-world problems using a structured process of empathizing, defining, ideating, prototyping, and testing. Look for opportunities to create human-centered innovations.

HYPERFOCUS AND FLOW

While hyperfocus can sometimes lead us down rabbit holes, it can also be an incredible asset when channeled intentionally. By harnessing your ability to enter a state of intense concentration and engagement, you can achieve remarkable productivity and mastery in your areas of interest. Some tips for leveraging hyperfocus:

- **Identify your passion projects:** What topics or activities fully engage your attention and energize you? Prioritize time for these pursuits, even if they don't feel "productive" in the conventional sense.
- **Create the right conditions:** Notice what environmental factors help you enter a state of flow, such as a certain type of music, a specific location, or a particular time of day. Aim to replicate these conditions when you need to tackle a challenging task.
- **Use a timer:** Set a timer for a focused work session, and challenge yourself to stay fully engaged until the timer goes off. Start with shorter intervals and gradually increase the duration as your focus muscle grows.
- **Leverage body doubling:** Enlist a study buddy or work partner to sit with you while you tackle a focus-intensive task. The mere presence of another person can help anchor your attention and reduce distractibility.

INTUITION AND PATTERN RECOGNITION

ADHD brains are often remarkably good at seeing patterns, making intuitive leaps, and sensing what's not being said. By learning to trust and refine your intuition, you can make better decisions, build stronger relationships, and spot opportunities others might overlook. Some ways to cultivate your intuitive abilities:

- **Practice metacognition:** Pay attention to your thought processes and the subtle cues your brain is picking up on. What hunches, gut feelings, or flashes of insight are you noticing? Keep a journal to track your intuitive hits and misses.
- **Ask powerful questions:** Hone your ability to ask penetrating, thought-provoking questions that get to the heart of the matter. Notice what patterns or themes emerge in the responses you receive.
- **Engage in mind-mapping:** Use visual tools like mind maps or concept maps to explore the connections and relationships between ideas. Look for patterns, gaps, or insights that emerge from this bird's-eye view.
- **Seek diverse perspectives:** Expose yourself to a wide range of viewpoints, experiences, and fields of knowledge. The more raw material you have to work with, the richer your pattern recognition abilities will be.

RESILIENCE AND ADAPTABILITY

Life with ADHD inevitably involves its fair share of setbacks, failures, and derailments. However, these challenges can also forge remarkable resilience and adaptability—the ability to bounce back from adversity, pivot when needed, and find creative solutions to seemingly intractable problems. Some ways to build your resilience muscle:

- **Reframe failure as learning:** Approach setbacks with curiosity rather than self-judgment. What can you learn from this experience? How can you apply these insights going forward?
- **Cultivate a growth mindset:** Embrace the belief that your abilities and intelligence can be developed through effort, learning, and persistence. Celebrate progress, not just outcomes.
- **Practice self-compassion:** Treat yourself with kindness and understanding when you stumble or struggle. Recognize that imperfection and adversity are part of the human experience.
- **Seek support:** Build a network of supportive friends, family members, mentors, and professionals who can offer encouragement, guidance, and perspective when times get tough.

ENERGY AND ENTHUSIASM

ADHD brains often have an abundance of energy, enthusiasm, and passion for the things that interest them. This zest for life can be contagious, inspiring and motivating those around you. Some ways to harness your energy and enthusiasm for good:

- **Pursue your passions:** Seek out work and hobbies that align with your natural interests and curiosities. When you're engaged in something you love, your energy and enthusiasm will be self-sustaining.
- **Lead by example:** Let your passion and commitment to your values shine through in your actions and interactions. Others will be drawn to your authenticity and conviction.
- **Spread positivity:** Look for opportunities to uplift and encourage those around you. Share your gratitude, offer sincere compliments, and celebrate others' successes.
- **Advocate for change:** Use your energy and enthusiasm to champion causes you care about. Whether it's volunteering for a local nonprofit or speaking out against injustice, your passion can be a powerful force for good.

By intentionally developing and applying your ADHD superpowers, you can not only overcome the challenges of this condition but also create a life of tremendous impact, fulfillment, and joy. Embrace your unique wiring, and use it to make a positive difference in your own life and the lives of those around you.

As we move into the next section of this book, we'll explore how to apply these strengths and strategies to specific areas of life, from academics and career to relationships and personal growth. With a solid foundation of self-awareness, practical skills, and positive habits, you'll be well-equipped to navigate the journey ahead. So let's dive in and start building a life that works with your ADHD, not against it.

Part III: Thriving in All Areas of Life

Armed with a deeper understanding of your ADHD brain and a toolkit of strategies for harnessing its potential, you're ready to start applying these insights to every area of your life. Whether you're navigating school, work, relationships, or personal pursuits, the key is to design your environment and approach to complement your natural wiring.

In this section, we'll explore evidence-based strategies and real-world tips for thriving with ADHD in all the major domains of life:

- **Academics:** How to excel in school by tailoring your study habits, time management, and self-advocacy to your unique learning style.
- **Career:** How to find a fulfilling vocation that aligns with your strengths and values, and how to navigate common workplace challenges with grace and grit.
- **Relationships:** How to cultivate deeper connections with family, friends, and romantic partners by honoring your needs, improving communication, and practicing empathy.
- **Lifestyle and Self-Care:** How to optimize your physical health, emotional well-being, and daily habits to reduce stress and increase resilience.

Throughout this section, we'll also highlight the power of self-advocacy and seeking support when needed. No one thrives in isolation, and part of living well with ADHD is learning to ask for help, accommodations, and understanding from those around you.

Remember, thriving with ADHD is an ongoing, iterative process. Progress is rarely linear, and setbacks are a normal part of the journey. Be patient with yourself, celebrate your victories along the way, and trust that every challenge is an opportunity for growth and self-discovery.

So let's dive in and start exploring how to create a life of meaning, connection, and joy – not in spite of your ADHD, but because of it. With the right mindset, tools, and support, there's no limit to what you can achieve.

ACADEMIC MASTERY: LEARNING ON YOUR OWN TERMS

For many people with ADHD, the classroom can feel like a minefield of challenges, from struggling to focus during lectures to pulling all-nighters to finish papers at the last minute. However, by better understanding your unique learning needs and advocating for accommodations, you can not only survive but thrive in your academic pursuits.

UNDERSTANDING YOUR LEARNING STYLE

Everyone learns differently, but for people with ADHD, finding the right learning strategies is especially crucial. Some common learning styles include:

- **Visual:** You learn best through diagrams, charts, videos, and other visual aids. Highlighters, color-coding, and mind-mapping are your friends.
- **Auditory:** You retain information well through listening and verbal discussion. Lectures, podcasts, and study groups may be particularly helpful.
- **Tactile:** You prefer hands-on learning experiences, like labs, simulations, and building models. Fidget toys and doodling can also help you stay focused.
- **Kinesthetic:** You learn by doing and moving. Taking frequent study breaks to stretch, walk, or do jumping jacks can help you stay alert and engaged.

Most people have a mix of learning styles, so experiment to find the combination that works best for you. Don't be afraid to try unconventional strategies, like listening to baroque music while studying or using a treadmill desk to read.

OPTIMIZING YOUR STUDY ENVIRONMENT

Where and how you study can make a big difference in your ability to focus and retain information. Some tips for creating an ADHD-friendly study space:

- **Minimize distractions:** Choose a quiet location away from high-traffic areas, turn off notifications on your devices, and use website blockers to avoid digital rabbit holes.
- **Incorporate movement:** Use a standing desk, sit on an exercise ball, or take frequent stretch breaks to keep your body and brain engaged.
- **Optimize your acoustics:** Experiment with white noise, nature sounds, or instrumental music to find the ideal background noise for focus. Noise-cancelling headphones can also be a gamechanger.
- **Consider your lighting:** Some people with ADHD find that bright, natural light helps them feel alert, while others prefer dimmer, warmer tones. Experiment to find your ideal lighting setup.

EFFECTIVE STUDY TECHNIQUES

In addition to optimizing your environment, adopting active, brain-friendly study strategies can help you absorb and retain information more effectively. Some techniques to try:

- **Pomodoro Method:** Set a timer for 25 minutes of focused work, followed by a 5-minute break. After 4 "pomodoros," take a longer break of 15-30 minutes. This helps maintain motivation and avoid burnout.
- **Chunking:** Break large projects or study sessions into smaller, more manageable chunks. This makes it easier to get started and maintain momentum.
- **Active recall:** Instead of just re-reading your notes, quiz yourself or teach the material to an imaginary audience. This forces your brain to actively engage with the information.
- **Spaced repetition:** Review material at increasing intervals (e.g., 1 day, 3 days, 7 days, etc.) to help transfer it from short-term to long-term memory. Flashcard apps like Anki use this principle.

TIME MANAGEMENT AND ORGANIZATION

Staying on top of deadlines, readings, and assignments is often the biggest challenge for ADHD students. Some strategies to keep yourself organized and on track:

- **Use a planner:** Whether it's a physical planner or a digital app like Google Calendar or Trello, having one central location for all your assignments and deadlines is crucial.
- **Break down big projects:** Use reverse-engineering to break large papers or projects into smaller, more manageable steps. Work backwards from the due date to create mini-deadlines for each stage.
- **Create routines:** Establish regular times for studying, exercise, meals, and sleep. A consistent schedule helps regulate your body's internal clock and makes it easier to focus.
- **Use visual reminders:** Place Post-It notes, wall calendars, or whiteboards in prominent locations to keep important deadlines and to-dos visible and top-of-mind.

SELF-ADVOCACY AND SUPPORT

Many colleges and universities offer accommodations for students with ADHD, such as extended time on tests, note-taking services, or reduced course loads. However, it's up to you to seek out these resources and advocate for your needs. Some tips:

- **Register with your school's disability services office:** Provide documentation of your ADHD diagnosis to access formal accommodations.
- **Communicate with your professors:** Let them know about your ADHD and what accommodations you need to succeed in their class. Most professors want to help, but they can't if they don't know.
- **Seek out study partners:** Collaborating with classmates can help keep you accountable and provide a source of social support. Look for people with complementary strengths.
- **Consider coaching or therapy:** Many campuses offer ADHD coaching or counseling services to help students develop academic and life skills. Don't be afraid to seek out this extra support.

Remember, academic success with ADHD is absolutely possible - it just may look different than the traditional path. By understanding your unique learning needs, advocating for accommodations, and using brain-friendly strategies, you can unlock your full potential as a student and lifelong learner.

Next, we'll explore how to translate these skills into the

professional world and build a fulfilling, successful career that aligns with your strengths and values. So let's dive in!

CAREER SUCCESS: FINDING YOUR NICHE AND THRIVING

For adults with ADHD, finding a career path that aligns with their unique strengths, interests, and needs can be a game-changer. The right job can provide a sense of purpose, engagement, and fulfillment that makes even the toughest days worthwhile. But how do you find that ideal fit? And once you do, how do you navigate common workplace challenges like time management, organization, and interpersonal communication?

IDENTIFYING YOUR PASSIONS AND STRENGTHS

The first step in building a satisfying career is getting clear on what you want and what you have to offer. Some questions to ask yourself:

- What activities make you lose track of time?
- What skills or talents come naturally to you?
- What problems do you enjoy solving?
- What topics could you talk about for hours?
- What work or volunteer experiences have been most fulfilling for you?

Look for common threads and themes in your answers. Are you drawn to creative pursuits like writing, design, or music? Do you thrive in fast-paced, high-pressure environments like emergency medicine or journalism? Do you have a knack for analyzing complex systems or solving technical problems?

In addition to self-reflection, seek input from friends, family, and mentors who know you well. What strengths and talents do they see in you? What careers do they think you'd excel in? Sometimes an outside perspective can illuminate possibilities you hadn't considered.

FINDING THE RIGHT FIT

Once you have a clearer sense of your passions and strengths, it's time to start exploring career paths that align with them. Some factors to consider:

- **Work environment:** Do you thrive in a structured, predictable setting or a more dynamic, flexible one? Do you prefer solo work or collaborating with a team?
- **Job duties:** What day-to-day tasks energize you? What drains you? Look for roles that maximize your strengths and minimize your pain points.
- **Company culture:** What values and management styles bring out your best? Seek out organizations that align with your needs and preferences.
- **Growth potential:** What opportunities for learning, advancement, and leadership excite you? Choose a path with room for you to grow and evolve.

Don't be afraid to think outside the box. Many adults with ADHD find fulfillment in unconventional careers like entrepreneurship, freelancing, or creative fields. The key is to find work that engages your unique brain and gives you a sense of meaning and purpose.

MANAGING TASKS AND PRIORITIES

Once you've landed a job you love (or at least like!), the next challenge is staying organized and productive amidst competing deadlines and distractions. Some strategies to try:

- **Break down projects into smaller steps:** Use a project management tool like Trello or Asana to chunk large assignments into more manageable sub-tasks.
- **Use time-blocking:** Schedule focused work sessions for your most important tasks, and protect that time fiercely. Use a timer or app to stay on track.
- **Prioritize ruthlessly:** Use the Eisenhower Matrix to distinguish between urgent and important tasks. Learn to say no to non-essential requests.
- **Automate and delegate:** Look for tasks that can be streamlined with technology or assigned to others. Don't be afraid to ask for help when you need it.

MAINTAINING FOCUS AND MOTIVATION

Staying focused and motivated can be a constant challenge for ADHD brains, especially when tasks are tedious or uninteresting. Some tips for staying on track:

- **Create external accountability:** Enlist a coworker or accountability partner to help you stay on task. Schedule regular check-ins to report on your progress.
- **Use positive reinforcement:** Reward yourself for completing difficult tasks or reaching milestones. Celebrate your wins, no matter how small.
- **Take regular breaks:** Use the Pomodoro technique or another timed break method to recharge your brain and avoid burnout. Get up and move around every 30-60 minutes.
- **Find your optimal working conditions:** Experiment with different environments, tools, and routines to find what helps you focus best. Don't be afraid to advocate for accommodations like a quiet workspace or flexible hours.

IMPROVING COMMUNICATION AND RELATIONSHIPS

ADHD can sometimes make interpersonal communication and relationships more challenging, both with coworkers and supervisors. Some tips for navigating these dynamics:

- **Practice active listening:** Make a conscious effort to focus on what others are saying, without interrupting or getting distracted. Repeat back key points to ensure understanding.
- **Think before you speak:** Take a moment to consider your words before blurting them out. If you tend to be impulsive, try writing down your thoughts first.
- **Be proactive in seeking feedback:** Don't wait for annual reviews to get input on your performance. Schedule regular check-ins with your supervisor to discuss your progress and areas for improvement.
- **Advocate for your needs:** If you're struggling with a particular task or situation, speak up and ask for help. Most managers want you to succeed, but they can't offer support if they don't know what you need.

Remember, building a successful career with ADHD is an ongoing process of self-discovery, experimentation, and growth. There will be triumphs and setbacks along the way - the key is to stay curious, adaptable, and committed to your own unique path.

By combining your passions and strengths with brain-friendly strategies for productivity, focus, and communication, you can not only find work you love, but excel at it. So keep exploring, advocating for yourself, and trusting in your own potential - your dream career is within reach.

Next, we'll explore how to cultivate thriving relationships with family, friends, and romantic partners by improving communication, managing emotions, and playing to your interpersonal strengths. Stay tuned!

HARMONIOUS RELATIONSHIPS: CONNECTING AUTHENTICALLY

Relationships can be a source of great joy, support, and personal growth - but they can also be a minefield of misunderstandings, hurt feelings, and unmet expectations. For adults with ADHD, the challenges of communication, emotional regulation, and consistency can make it even harder to navigate the complexities of human connection.

However, by understanding how your ADHD affects your relationships, practicing new skills and strategies, and choosing partners who appreciate your unique qualities, you absolutely can cultivate deep, fulfilling bonds with others. Let's explore some key principles and techniques for thriving in your interpersonal relationships.

UNDERSTANDING HOW ADHD AFFECTS RELATIONSHIPS

The first step in improving your relationships is getting clear on how your ADHD symptoms and traits may be impacting your interactions with others. Some common challenges include:

- **Communication:** You may tend to interrupt, blurt out thoughts without a filter, or zone out during conversations, leading to misunderstandings and frustration.
- **Emotional regulation:** Impulsivity, low frustration tolerance, and rejection sensitivity can make it harder to manage conflicts and maintain emotional balance in relationships.
- **Consistency:** Difficulty with follow-through, time management, and remembering commitments can strain trust and reliability in partnerships.
- **Listening and empathy:** Distractibility and inattention can make it harder to tune in to others' needs and feelings, leading to a sense of disconnection.

Of course, ADHD can also bring many positive qualities to relationships, such as creativity, spontaneity, passion, and a fresh perspective. The key is to balance leveraging your strengths with developing skills to manage your challenges.

CULTIVATING SELF-AWARENESS AND RESPONSIBILITY

One of the most important relationship skills you can develop is self-awareness - the ability to recognize your own patterns, triggers, and impacts on others. Some practices to build your self-awareness muscle:

- **Reflect on past interactions:** After a difficult conversation or conflict, take some time to replay what happened in your mind. What triggered you? How did you respond? What might you do differently next time?
- **Ask for feedback:** Invite trusted friends, family members, or your partner to share their honest perceptions of your communication style, emotional responses, and reliability. Listen with an open mind, and focus on understanding rather than defending.
- **Notice your physical cues:** Start to tune into the physical sensations that precede emotional reactions, like a racing heart, tense muscles, or shallow breathing. These can be early warning signs that you need to pause and regroup.
- **Take ownership of your actions:** When you make a mistake or let someone down, resist the urge to blame or make excuses. Acknowledge your role, apologize sincerely, and commit to making amends.

Self-awareness is the foundation for taking responsibility for your impacts on others and making positive changes in your relationships. It's an ongoing, lifelong practice - but one that gets easier with time and effort.

IMPROVING COMMUNICATION AND EMOTIONAL CONNECTION

Effective communication is the lifeblood of any healthy relationship. Some strategies for improving your communication and deepening your emotional connections:

- **Practice active listening:** When your partner or friend is speaking, give them your full attention. Make eye contact, put away distractions, and focus on understanding their perspective. Reflect back what you heard to ensure clarity.
- **Use "I" statements:** When expressing your own thoughts and feelings, start with "I" rather than "you." For example, "I feel hurt when you cancel our plans at the last minute" instead of "You always flake on me." This helps prevent defensiveness.
- **Ask open-ended questions:** Show genuine curiosity about others' experiences and perspectives. Ask questions that invite elaboration, like "What was that like for you?" or "How did you feel when that happened?"
- **Express appreciation:** Make a habit of noticing and commenting on the positive qualities and actions of your loved ones. Gratitude and admiration are powerful relationship glue.

GERTRUDESWANSON

Remember, good communication is a two-way street. It's not just about expressing yourself effectively, but also creating space for others to feel heard and understood.

MANAGING DIFFICULT EMOTIONS AND CONFLICTS

Emotional dysregulation and impulsivity can be major stumbling blocks in ADHD relationships. Some tips for managing strong emotions and navigating conflicts:

- **Identify your triggers:** Notice the situations, words, or dynamics that tend to spark big emotional reactions for you. Develop a plan for how to respond more skillfully in those moments.
- **Take a time-out:** If you feel yourself getting overwhelmed or reactive, it's okay to take a break. Let your partner know you need some time to calm down, and commit to returning to the conversation when you're in a better headspace.
- **Practice self-soothing:** Experiment with techniques like deep breathing, progressive muscle relaxation, or visualizing a peaceful scene to help regulate your body and emotions.
- **Seek professional help:** If you're struggling with chronic anger, anxiety, or mood swings, consider working with a therapist who specializes in ADHD and relationships. They can help you develop additional coping strategies.

Conflict is a normal part of any relationship - it's how you navigate it that matters. By taking responsibility for your own emotions, communicating with care and respect, and being willing to compromise and apologize, you can turn conflicts into opportunities for growth and connection.

BUILDING TRUST AND RELIABILITY

One of the most common complaints in ADHD relationships is a lack of follow-through and reliability. Some ways to build trust and demonstrate your commitment:

- **Use external reminders:** Rely on calendars, alarms, and to-do lists to help you remember important dates, tasks, and commitments. Share your system with your partner so they know you're on top of things.
- **Break big promises into smaller chunks:** If you're prone to overcommitting or underestimating how long things will take, try breaking big promises into more manageable steps. Communicate your progress along the way.
- **Prioritize your partner:** Make a conscious effort to put your relationship first, even when life gets hectic. Show up for the things that matter most to your partner, like date nights, family events, or crucial conversations.
- **Rebuild after setbacks:** When you do let your partner down, take full responsibility and make amends. Ask what they need to feel secure and prioritized, and follow through consistently to rebuild trust over time.

No one is perfect, and slip-ups are bound to happen. The key is to communicate openly, repair ruptures quickly, and keep showing up for your relationship with renewed commitment.

By combining self-awareness, effective communication, emotional regulation skills, and a dedication to reliability, you can absolutely build strong, healthy bonds with the most important people in your life. It takes patience, practice, and perseverance - but the rewards of true intimacy and connection are more than worth it.

Next, we'll explore how to optimize your physical health, emotional well-being, and daily habits to reduce stress, increase focus, and build the resilience needed to bounce back from any challenge that comes your way. The journey continues!

MASTERING THE EVERYDAY: FROM FINANCES TO FITNESS

Life with ADHD can often feel like a constant juggling act, with countless balls in the air at any given time. Between managing your health, keeping up with household chores, staying on top of bills and budgets, and finding time for self-care and fun, it's easy to feel overwhelmed and stretched thin.

However, by implementing some key strategies and habits, you can absolutely learn to master the everyday demands of adult life and create more space for what truly matters to you. Let's explore some practical tips and techniques for optimizing your daily routines and building a strong foundation for overall well-being.

CREATING A BUDGET AND FINANCIAL PLAN

Financial stress is a common challenge for adults with ADHD, who may struggle with impulsivity, forgetfulness, and organization when it comes to money matters. Some tips for getting your finances in order:

- **Track your spending:** For one month, write down every penny you spend, from bills to daily coffee runs. Categorize your expenses to get a clear picture of where your money is going.
- **Create a budget:** Based on your tracking, identify areas where you can cut back or reallocate funds. Use a budgeting app like Mint or YNAB to help you stay on track.
- **Set financial goals:** Identify short-term and long-term financial goals, like paying off debt, saving for a big purchase, or building an emergency fund. Break these down into manageable steps and celebrate your progress along the way.
- **Automate your savings and bills:** Set up automatic transfers to your savings account and use online bill pay to ensure you never miss a due date. Remove the friction and remember to make smart financial choices.
- **Find an accountability partner:** Enlist a trusted friend, family member, or financial coach to help you stay on track and make sound decisions. Schedule regular check-ins to review your progress and troubleshoot challenges.

Remember, getting your finances in order is a process, not an overnight fix. Be patient with yourself, celebrate your wins, and keep focusing on your long-term vision of financial health and freedom.

ORGANIZING YOUR HOME AND WORKSPACE

A cluttered, chaotic environment can exacerbate ADHD symptoms and make it harder to focus, relax, and get things done. Some strategies for creating more order and ease in your physical space:

- **Start small:** Choose one drawer, shelf, or corner to declutter and organize at a time. Set a timer for 15-20 minutes and see how much you can accomplish in that short burst.
- **Create designated homes for items:** Assign specific places for things like keys, mail, and important documents. Label shelves and containers to make it easy to find what you need and put things back where they belong.
- **Use visual cues:** Color-code files, use clear storage containers, or hang important reminders on the wall to make information more visually accessible and memorable.
- **Purge regularly:** Set a quarterly or annual reminder to go through your belongings and let go of anything that's no longer serving you. Donate, recycle, or sell items you no longer need or use.
- **Enlist help:** If organizing isn't your strong suit, consider hiring a professional organizer for a jumpstart or ongoing support. You can also trade organizing favors with a friend or family member who enjoys this kind of task.

Remember, the goal isn't to achieve perfect, magazine-worthy organization, but rather to create a functional, livable space that supports your daily activities and reduces stress and overwhelm.

PRIORITIZING SELF-CARE AND WELLNESS

When life gets hectic, self-care is often the first thing to fall by the wayside. But for adults with ADHD, prioritizing your physical and mental health is absolutely essential for managing symptoms, improving focus and mood, and avoiding burnout. Some non-negotiables to build into your routine:

- **Get enough sleep:** Aim for 7-9 hours per night, with a consistent sleep and wake time. Create a calming bedtime routine, limit screentime before bed, and keep your bedroom cool, dark, and quiet.
- **Eat regular, nourishing meals:** Fuel your brain and body with plenty of protein, healthy fats, fruits, and vegetables. Limit sugary, processed foods that can cause energy crashes and brain fog.
- **Move your body daily:** Find physical activities that you enjoy and that get your heart rate up, like brisk walking, dancing, swimming, or cycling. Aim for at least 30 minutes per day, broken up into shorter chunks if needed.
- **Practice mindfulness:** Incorporate calming, focusing practices into your daily routine, like meditation, deep breathing, yoga, or time in nature. Start small, with just a few minutes per day, and build up over time.
- **Nurture your passions:** Make time for hobbies, interests, and activities that light you up and bring you joy. Prioritize these as much as you would any other important commitment.

Self-care isn't selfish - it's a crucial foundation for showing up fully in all areas of your life. Treat your wellness as a non-negotiable priority, and watch as your focus, energy, and resilience grow.

SEEKING PROFESSIONAL SUPPORT

Sometimes, despite our best efforts at implementing helpful strategies and habits, we can still feel stuck or overwhelmed. If you find yourself struggling to manage your ADHD symptoms, emotions, or life demands, it may be time to seek professional support. Some options to consider:

- **Therapy:** Working with a mental health professional who specializes in ADHD can be incredibly helpful for developing coping strategies, processing emotions, and overcoming obstacles. Look for a therapist who uses evidence-based approaches like cognitive-behavioral therapy (CBT) or dialectical behavior therapy (DBT).
- **ADHD coaching:** An ADHD coach can help you develop practical skills and strategies for managing your time, tasks, and goals. They provide accountability, support, and guidance as you work towards your vision of success.
- **Medication:** For some people, medication can be a helpful tool for managing ADHD symptoms in combination with therapy and lifestyle changes. Work with a qualified healthcare provider to explore your options and find the right fit for you.
- **Support groups:** Connecting with others who understand the challenges and triumphs of life with ADHD can be incredibly validating and empowering. Look for local or

online support groups through organizations like CHADD or ADDA.

Remember, seeking help is a sign of strength, not weakness. By advocating for your needs and building a supportive team, you set yourself up for long-term success and well-being.

Mastering the everyday demands of adult life with ADHD is an ongoing process of trial and error, self-discovery, and growth. By implementing practical strategies, building healthy habits, and reaching out for support when needed, you can absolutely create a life that works with your brain, not against it.

In the next section, we'll dive deeper into the various treatment options available for adult ADHD, from traditional approaches like medication and therapy to alternative interventions like nutrition, exercise, and mindfulness. Armed with this knowledge, you'll be empowered to create a personalized plan for optimal symptom management and well-being. The best is yet to come!

ADHD TREATMENT: FINDING WHAT WORKS FOR YOU

Just as no two people with ADHD are exactly alike, there's no one-size-fits-all approach to treating this complex condition. The most effective treatment plans are tailored to your unique needs, goals, and preferences, and often involve a combination of strategies and interventions.

In this chapter, we'll explore the most common and well-researched treatment options for adult ADHD, from conventional approaches like medication and therapy to alternative interventions like nutrition, exercise, and mindfulness. We'll also discuss how to work with professionals to create a personalized plan that fits your lifestyle and empowers you to thrive.

CONVENTIONAL TREATMENT OPTIONS

When most people think of ADHD treatment, they often think of medication first. While medication can be a highly effective tool for managing symptoms, it's not the only option, and it's not right for everyone. Let's take a closer look at the most common conventional treatments for adult ADHD.

STIMULANT MEDICATION

Stimulant medications like methylphenidate (Ritalin, Concerta) and amphetamines (Adderall, Vyvanse) are the most widely prescribed treatments for ADHD. They work by increasing the availability of dopamine and norepinephrine in the brain, which can improve focus, impulse control, and task persistence.

Pros:

- Rapid symptom relief, often within hours of taking the first dose
- Highly effective for most people with ADHD, with a response rate of 70-80%
- Can improve not only core ADHD symptoms but also related issues like emotional dysregulation and restlessness

Cons:

- Potential side effects like appetite loss, sleep disturbances, anxiety, and irritability
- Risk of abuse or dependence, especially with short-acting formulations
- Not suitable for people with certain medical conditions like heart problems or a history of substance abuse

If you and your doctor decide to try stimulant medication, it's important to start at a low dose and titrate up slowly to find the optimal balance of benefits and side effects. Regular check-ins with your prescriber are essential to monitor your response and make any necessary adjustments.

NON-STIMULANT MEDICATION

For people who can't tolerate stimulants or who don't respond well to them, non-stimulant medications like atomoxetine (Strattera), guanfacine (Intuniv), and clonidine (Kapvay) may be an option. These medications work by targeting different neurotransmitter systems in the brain, such as norepinephrine and alpha-2 receptors.

Pros:

- Lower risk of abuse or dependence compared to stimulants
- Can be a good option for people with comorbid anxiety or tics
- May have a smoother, more sustained effect throughout the day

Cons:

- Slower onset of action, often taking several weeks to reach full effect
- Lower response rates compared to stimulants, around 40-60%
- Potential side effects like fatigue, nausea, dry mouth, and dizziness

Non-stimulant medications are often used as a second-line treatment when stimulants are not tolerated or effective, or as an adjunct to stimulants for additional symptom control.

THERAPY

While medication can be highly effective for managing ADHD symptoms, it doesn't teach coping strategies or address the emotional and social impacts of living with ADHD. That's where therapy comes in. Several types of therapy have been shown to be effective for adults with ADHD, including:

- **Cognitive-Behavioral Therapy (CBT):** CBT helps you identify and change negative thought patterns and behaviors that may be exacerbating your ADHD symptoms. You'll learn practical skills for managing time, organizing tasks, and coping with emotions.
- **Dialectical Behavior Therapy (DBT):** DBT is a type of CBT that emphasizes mindfulness, distress tolerance, and emotion regulation. It can be particularly helpful for adults with ADHD who struggle with impulsivity, mood swings, or interpersonal conflicts.
- **Psychoeducation:** Learning about ADHD and how it affects your brain and behavior can be incredibly empowering. Psychoeducation helps you understand your strengths and challenges, communicate your needs to others, and advocate for yourself in work and relationships.
- **Couples or Family Therapy:** ADHD can have a significant impact on relationships, leading to misunderstandings, resentments, and power struggles. Couples or family therapy can help you and your loved ones learn to communicate better, distribute responsibilities fairly, and rebuild trust and intimacy.

Therapy is most effective when it's tailored to your specific needs and goals, and when you have a strong rapport with your therapist. Don't hesitate to shop around until you find a good fit, and be open and honest about your challenges and progress along the way.

ALTERNATIVE TREATMENT OPTIONS

In addition to medication and therapy, there are many alternative or complementary approaches that can support your overall well-being and help you manage ADHD symptoms. While the research on these interventions is still emerging, many people with ADHD find them to be valuable tools in their treatment toolkit.

LIFESTYLE MODIFICATIONS

Making targeted changes to your daily habits and routines can have a big impact on your ADHD symptoms and overall quality of life. Some key areas to focus on:

- **Sleep:** Aim for 7-9 hours per night, with a consistent sleep and wake schedule. Create a calming bedtime routine and optimize your sleep environment for comfort and relaxation.
- **Exercise:** Regular physical activity boosts dopamine and norepinephrine levels in the brain, which can improve focus, mood, and impulse control. Aim for at least 30 minutes of moderate exercise most days of the week.
- **Nutrition:** Eating a balanced, nutrient-dense diet can help stabilize blood sugar, reduce inflammation, and support healthy brain function. Some people with ADHD also find that limiting caffeine, sugar, and artificial additives can improve their symptoms.
- **Stress management:** Chronic stress can worsen ADHD symptoms and lead to burnout. Incorporate regular stress-reducing activities into your routine, like meditation, deep breathing, yoga, or time in nature.

MINDFULNESS AND MEDITATION

Mindfulness is the practice of paying attention to the present moment with openness, curiosity, and non-judgment. Research suggests that mindfulness meditation can help improve attention, emotion regulation, and self-awareness in people with ADHD.

There are many ways to practice mindfulness, from formal seated meditation to more informal practices like mindful eating or walking. Apps like Headspace, Calm, or Insight Timer can be a great way to get started with guided meditations and short daily practices.

OMEGA-3 FATTY ACIDS

Omega-3 fatty acids, particularly EPA and DHA, are essential for healthy brain function and development. Some studies have found that supplementing with omega-3s can improve ADHD symptoms like inattention, hyperactivity, and impulsivity, though more research is needed.

Good food sources of omega-3s include fatty fish like salmon, sardines, and anchovies, as well as flaxseeds, chia seeds, and walnuts. If you choose to take an omega-3 supplement, look for a reputable brand that tests for purity and potency, and talk to your doctor about the appropriate dosage for your needs.

NEUROFEEDBACK

Neurofeedback is a type of brain training that uses real-time feedback from EEG sensors to help you learn to regulate your brain activity. The goal is to increase the ratio of beta (focused, alert) to theta (drowsy, distracted) brainwaves, which can lead to improved attention, impulse control, and emotional stability.

During a neurofeedback session, you'll wear a sensor cap and play a video game or watch a movie while your brain activity is monitored. The game or movie will only play when your brain is in the desired state, providing instant feedback and rewards for focused attention.

While more research is needed to confirm the long-term efficacy of neurofeedback for ADHD, many people report significant improvements in their symptoms and overall functioning after a course of treatment.

BUILDING YOUR TREATMENT PLAN

With so many treatment options available, it can be overwhelming to know where to start. The key is to work closely with your healthcare providers to create a personalized plan that fits your unique needs, preferences, and lifestyle.

Here are some steps to get started:

1. **Get a comprehensive evaluation:** Start by getting a thorough assessment from a qualified mental health professional, such as a psychiatrist, psychologist, or neuropsychologist who specializes in ADHD. They can help you get an accurate diagnosis, identify any co-occurring conditions, and develop a targeted treatment plan.
2. **Educate yourself:** Learn as much as you can about ADHD and the various treatment options available. Read books, articles, and blogs from reputable sources, and connect with others who have ADHD to learn from their experiences.
3. **Set clear goals:** Work with your treatment team to identify specific, measurable goals for your treatment, such as improving your time management skills, reducing procrastination, or improving your relationships. Having clear objectives can help you track your progress and stay motivated.
4. **Start with the basics:** Before diving into more intensive interventions, make sure you have a solid foundation

of self-care in place. Prioritize sleep, nutrition, exercise, and stress management, and build these habits into your daily routine.
5. **Consider medication:** If your symptoms are significantly impacting your daily functioning, talk to your doctor about whether medication might be right for you. Be open and honest about your concerns and preferences, and work together to find the optimal type and dosage for your needs.
6. **Engage in therapy:** Look for a therapist who specializes in ADHD and uses evidence-based approaches like CBT or DBT. Be an active participant in your sessions, and practice your new skills and strategies between appointments.
7. **Experiment with alternative approaches:** Incorporate mindfulness, omega-3s, or other complementary strategies into your treatment plan, and pay attention to how they impact your symptoms and overall well-being. Be patient and persistent, as it may take time to find the right combination of approaches for you.
8. **Enlist support:** Build a strong support system of family, friends, and professionals who understand ADHD and can offer encouragement, accountability, and practical help when needed. Consider joining a support group or working with an ADHD coach for additional guidance and motivation.

Remember, finding the right treatment plan is an ongoing process of trial and error, self-discovery, and adjustment. What works for you today may need to be tweaked or overhauled as your needs and circumstances change.

The most important thing is to stay curious, compassionate, and committed to your own well-being. With patience, persistence, and a willingness to experiment, you can absolutely find a treatment approach that empowers you to thrive with ADHD.

CONCLUSION: THE JOURNEY CONTINUES

Throughout this book, we've explored the many facets of living well with adult ADHD – from understanding the science behind your symptoms to implementing practical strategies for productivity, relationships, and self-care. We've busted myths, celebrated strengths, and offered a roadmap for turning ADHD from a liability into an asset.

But as you've likely gathered by now, thriving with ADHD is not a one-time event or a finite destination. It's an ongoing, lifelong journey of growth, self-discovery, and adaptation. Just as your brain is constantly evolving and your circumstances are always shifting, your approach to managing ADHD must also be flexible and responsive.

So as we come to the end of this book, I invite you to reflect on how far you've come – and how far you still want to go. What new insights, strategies, or mindset shifts have been most impactful for you? What areas of your life still feel like a struggle, and what kind of support do you need to move forward?

Remember, progress is rarely linear, and setbacks are a normal part of the journey. There will be days when you feel like you're crushing it, and others when you feel like you're barely keeping your head above water. The key is to approach each day with curiosity, compassion, and a commitment to small, consistent actions that move you closer to your goals.

Here are a few key principles to keep in mind as you continue on your path:

- **Embrace iteration:** Let go of the idea that you have to find the perfect system or solution right out of the gate. Instead, approach life with an experimental mindset, and be willing to try new things, learn from your missteps, and course-correct as needed.
- **Prioritize self-care:** Your physical, mental, and emotional well-being are the foundation for everything else in your life. Make time for activities that nourish your body, mind, and spirit, and don't be afraid to put your own oxygen mask on first.
- **Cultivate self-compassion:** Treat yourself with the same kindness, understanding, and forgiveness you would extend to a good friend. Recognize that everyone makes mistakes and has room for improvement, and that your worth is not contingent on your productivity or success.
- **Celebrate your successes:** Take time to acknowledge and savor your victories, no matter how small. Keeping a gratitude journal or sharing your wins with a supportive friend can help you stay motivated and focused on your progress.
- **Seek connection:** Build a network of supportive people who understand and accept you, ADHD and all. Reach out for help when you need it, and offer your own insights and encouragement to others on a similar path.
- **Keep learning:** Stay curious about the latest research, tools, and strategies for living well with ADHD. Read books and articles, listen to podcasts, attend conferences or workshops – and most importantly, keep experimenting to find what works for you.

Above all, remember that you are so much more than your ADHD. Yes, it's an important part of who you are, and learning to work with your unique brain wiring is key to unlocking your full potential. But it's not the only thing that defines you.

You are also a person with inherent worth, dignity, and agency. You have your own passions, values, and dreams, and you deserve to pursue them on your own terms. You have gifts to share with the world, and the capacity to make a difference in the lives of others.

So as you continue on your ADHD journey, keep your eyes on the bigger picture. Use the insights and strategies in this book as tools to help you navigate the terrain, but don't forget to look up and take in the view.

Embrace your quirks, celebrate your strengths, and never stop seeking ways to learn, grow, and thrive. With curiosity, compassion, and a commitment to your own unique path, there's no limit to what you can achieve.

Here's to the next chapter of your ADHD adventure – may it be filled with joy, purpose, and the realization of your wildest dreams.

ADDITIONAL RESOURCES

If you're looking to dive deeper into the topics covered in this book, or seeking additional support on your ADHD journey, here are some recommended resources to explore:

Books

- *Driven to Distraction* by Edward M. Hallowell and John J. Ratey
- *Taking Charge of Adult ADHD* by Russell A. Barkley
- *The Disorganized Mind* by Nancy A. Ratey
- *More Attention, Less Deficit* by Ari Tuckman
- *The ADHD Effect on Marriage* by Melissa Orlov
- *The Queen of Distraction* by Terry Matlen

Websites

- ADDitude Magazine (https://www.additudemag.com/) - Online magazine with articles, webinars, and resources for living well with ADHD
- CHADD (https://chadd.org/) - National non-profit organization providing education, advocacy, and support for people with ADHD
- ADD Resources (https://addresources.org/) - Non-profit organization offering information, resources, and networking opportunities for adults with ADHD
- Attention Deficit Disorder Association (https://add.org/) - Non-profit organization providing information, resources,

and support for adults with ADHD
- How to ADHD (https://howtoadhd.com/) - Website and YouTube channel by Jessica McCabe offering tips, tools, and insights for living well with ADHD

Podcasts

- ADHD reWired with Eric Tivers
- Taking Control: The ADHD Podcast with Nikki Kinzer and Pete Wright
- Distraction with Dr. Ned Hallowell
- ADHD Essentials with Brendan Mahan
- ADHD for Smart Ass Women with Tracy Otsuka

Coaching and Therapy Directory

- CHADD Professional Directory (https://chadd.org/professional-directory/) - Searchable directory of ADHD coaches, therapists, and other professionals
- ADDA Professional Directory (https://add.org/professional-directory/) - Searchable directory of ADHD coaches, therapists, and other professionals
- ADDitude Directory (https://directory.additudemag.com/) - Searchable directory of ADHD professionals, clinics, and centers

Support Groups and Communities

- CHADD Chapter Network (https://chadd.org/affiliate-locator/) - Searchable directory of local CHADD chapters and support groups
- ADDA Virtual Support Groups (https://add.org/virtual-support-groups/) - Free, online peer support groups for adults with ADHD
- ADHD Women's Palooza Facebook Group (https://www.facebook.com/groups/ADHDWomensPalooza) - Online community for women with ADHD

- /r/ADHD Subreddit (https://www.reddit.com/r/ADHD/) - Online forum for people with ADHD to share experiences, ask questions, and offer support

Remember, seeking out additional information and support is not a sign of weakness, but a powerful step towards self-advocacy and empowerment. By connecting with others who understand your struggles and triumphs, you can gain new insights, tools, and strategies for living well with ADHD.

So don't be afraid to reach out, ask for help, and tap into the wealth of resources available to you. With the right knowledge, tools, and support, you can absolutely create a life of meaning, purpose, and joy - not in spite of your ADHD, but because of it.

Here's to your ongoing growth, healing, and self-discovery - may this be just the beginning of a lifelong journey towards wholeness, resilience, and unapologetic authenticity.

Disclaimer

This book is intended for informational purposes only and should not be construed as professional advice. The information contained herein is not a substitute for professional guidance from qualified individuals in the relevant fields.

You are advised to consult with appropriate professionals, including but not limited to:

- **Healthcare professionals** for any health-related matters.
- **Business professionals** for financial, legal, or business advice.
- **Other relevant experts** in any field related to the topics discussed in this book.

The author and publisher make no warranties or representations, express or implied, with respect to the accuracy, completeness, or timeliness of the information contained in this book. The author and publisher disclaim all liability for any loss or damage resulting from the use or reliance on the information presented in this book.

This book is provided "as is" and without warranty of any kind, express or implied, including but not limited to warranties of merchantability, fitness for a particular purpose, and non-infringement.

It is your responsibility to independently verify any information presented in this book and seek professional advice as needed.

For other books and resources that may interest you, please click here:

Made in the USA
Monee, IL
05 March 2025